BRITAIN IN OLD PH

GRANTHAM

MALCOLM G. KNAPP

SUTTON PUBLISHING LIMITED

Sutton Publishing Limited
Phoenix Mill · Far Thrupp · Stroud
Gloucestershire · GL5 2BU

First published 1996

British Library Cataloguing in Publication Data

A catalogue record for this book is available from the British Library.

ISBN 0-7509-0801-7

Typeset in 10/12 Perpetua.
Typesetting and origination by
Sutton Publishing Limited.
Printed in Great Britain by
Ebenezer Baylis, Worcester.

To my parents, William Gerald Knapp (1902–70) and Doris Elizabeth Knapp (1901–94), and my sister Gillian (1934–60) whose life was cut so tragically short. They are remembered in this book.

A busy Saturday Market, when the sale of pigs was a great attraction to children of all ages. Notice how the church still continues to dominate the scene. This is wide Westgate and fortunately the 'planners' have not destroyed it. Each week a Saturday midday sale took place at the right of the picture. The crowd of people may indicate that it is taking place at the time of the photograph.

INTRODUCTION

I make no apology for trying to emphasize in this book the two aspects of Grantham's history that have not yet been fully explored. I also argue that had it not been for the arrival of Richard Hornsby in the early nineteenth century, Grantham would have remained a small market town and it would not have expanded as it did into the important centre for heavy and precision engineering that it became up until the recession of the 1980s. This success in engineering was the reason for the town's great increase in size and population in the 1800s, mainly because of Richard Hornsby's busy factory in Spittlegate which manufactured all types of agricultural and farming equipment, including steam and oil engines. Prior to that busy factory's arrival, the town had only two forms of communication with the outside world, the canal of the 1790s and the Great North Road. Then the railways came to town and I am positive this is because of the trade engendered by Hornsby's. Firstly the line to Nottingham opened in 1850 and this was followed two years later by the Great Northern Railway. This development created a previously unimagined opportunity to travel; to London, York and around the rest of England.

Engineering was of paramount importance to Grantham and yet it has not been fully investigated, researched or published. There have been informative booklets on Richard Hornsby and Ruston & Hornsby, both by Michael Pointer. Ruston & Hornsby alone has been the subject of a larger book, but that dealt mainly with the Lincoln factory. Both Aveling-Barford and Coles Cranes published publicity booklets years ago, but they were for their staff and were not readily available to the general public. As far as I can ascertain, such firms as B. Marco, the Ministry of Aircraft Production (a wartime company), Barrett Packaging, R.H. Neal, Potters Pumps, VacuLug, Grantham Boiler & Crank, Wisemans, Newmans and Coultas have nothing readily available in print on their history and importance to the development of engineering in Grantham. I understand that research is being carried out on B. Marco by Vaughan Hardy in the hope of publication, and Mary Lamyman has done much research into the Coultas family, so perhaps all is not lost.

It is vital that we all remember that Grantham almost completely owes its present existence and success to engineering, much of which has disappeared since the start of the 1980s. It is ironic that the closing down of so much of Grantham's industrial base occurred when a Grantham lady, Margaret Thatcher, was prime minister. Even the railway, which has been written about, has shrunk from a work force of about 400 to probably a lot less than 50.

The second subject to receive my attention is the role of education in the town, and one person in particular deserves special mention. She taught thousands of Grantham children at two local schools, Welby Street and Earlesfield County Primary. She may also have been a relief teacher at the Wharf Road Wesleyan School. I am, of course, referring to Nellie Frances Cant, later Mrs N.F. Brown and later still Mrs N.F. Goldner. I was one of the very first junior pupils at the newly built Earlesfield School in 1938 and Miss Cant transferred from the Welby Street School to open up the new school as head mistress. In fact she was never my teacher, but an enormous number of Grantham boys and girls were taught by her. As far as I can recall she was firm but fair.

Nellie Frances Cant was born in Swinegate in 1901 – she was a Victorian by a few weeks. When she died in February 1994 she was sadly not in her beloved Grantham or even in Lincolnshire, but at a nursing home in Leicestershire. The United Kingdom was big enough for her and she never holidayed abroad – the thought of an air flight or a sea voyage certainly did not appeal. After her education at the Fernside School on St Peter's Hill, then Kesteven & Grantham Girls School and finally Bishop Grosseteste College at Lincoln, she spent all her working life teaching Grantham's young children. Perhaps she was fortunate to retire before the great educational changes of recent years had even been thought of.

When I was asked to prepare this book it was suggested that all the photographs used should not have been published before. Bearing in mind that Michael Pointer and I have already produced a series of booklets entitled 'Bygone Grantham' and other books on Grantham have been published, all with old photographs, that was going to be a tall order. However, I am sure I have very nearly managed it, and the vast majority of the photographs published here have not seen the light of day before now. To my knowledge, well over 700 old photographs are already in print, so that with the publication of this book Grantham's past is well documented in photographic form. In order to find so many previously unpublished photographs, I have had to rely on the help of other photographers, postcard collectors and enthusiasts, and they are all gratefully acknowledged. If this book spurs on more local people to write a book or a pamphlet on another aspect of our town's history, then all my research, writing, compiling and checking will have been really worth while.

Finally I must add a note on the spelling of Spittlegate or Spitalgate. Until recently, both spellings were used, and in my text I have followed the spelling on the original document or picture. At the present time Spittlegate is the accepted spelling.

ACKNOWLEDGEMENTS

I gratefully acknowledge all the help given to me during the preparation of this book. First and foremost I would like to thank Nita, my wife, who has almost always patiently supervised my two-fingered exercises on her beloved word processor. For the loan of their treasured photographs I am very grateful to Zena Johnson and John Newman, once again, and to Mary Selby, Ron Haddock, Alf Kitchen and Peter Spalding for the first time of asking. I would also like to thank the following photographers: Doreen Houghton, *Boaz*, Laurence Bond, Don Brandom, John Caunt, Lewis Gerrard, Paul Girdlestone, Stefan Goldner, Malcolm Knapp, Walter Lee, John Mackay, Lt. Col. James Mandigo USAAF (rtd), John Oxby, Terry Shelbourne, F.G. Simpson and Chris Windows. If I have missed anyone out, then I apologize.

BIBLIOGRAPHY

Grantham Journal
Harrison's Almanacs, various years.
White and Kelly Directories.
The History of Kesteven & Grantham Girl's School, 1910–1987, Amy C. Old, 1988.
Grantham. The War Years. 1939–1945, Malcolm Knapp, 1995.
Grantham. A Pictorial History, Malcolm Knapp. 1990.
The Granthamian, The King's School, Summer 1946.
The Origin and Development of Aveling-Barford Limited, 1952.

St John's Church was built in 1841 in the expanding parish of Spittlegate (also spelt Spitalgate). The industry of Grantham was established in this area and was the cause of Grantham's great expansion both in size and population in the nineteenth century.

St Anne's Church in the parish of New Somerby. This parish was brought into 'Greater Grantham' in 1879 and the present church was built during the years 1906–9, replacing the 'tin tabernacle' in Cecil Street. The foundation stone was laid by Bishop Edward King Lincoln. St Anne's Iron Mission Church was opened in January 1884.

Just after the Second World War was over, the
spire of St Wulfram's Church was found to be in
great need of repair. That gave adventurous
photographers the chance of taking pictures
never snapped before, and this view of the spire
is one of them.

A delightful medieval face peering down over
Grantham, photographed during the necessary
repairs in 1947 when useful scaffolding and
ladders were in position.

Avenue Road, Grantham

Built during 1869–70 as the Congregational Church, this is now the United Reformed Church. It was one of the many important buildings erected in the fast expanding town during the Victorian era. Schools and churches were needed to cater for the rapidly increasing population. This postcard was mailed in 1911.

Wharf Road. This photograph was taken before the alterations were made to the front of the Baptist Church in 1930. The Public or Slipper Baths are next to the church and were demolished when the Isaac Newton shopping centre was built. The Baptist Church was opened in January 1864 and the Public Baths in August 1854.

RUSTON &
HORNSBY LTD.
OF
LINCOLN AND GRANTHAM

Britain's Largest Builders
of Oil Engines

Builders of Successful Oil Engines
since 1892

A Ruston & Hornsby catalogue cover. The claim to be Britain's largest builders of oil engines was probably correct.

As mentioned in the introduction, it is the aim of this book to emphasize the former heavy industry and engineering of Grantham. The next few photographs, never published before, were taken in the factory of Richard Hornsby in the early twentieth century. This is of No. 12 Shop, the oil engine erecting shop.

The drilling section of No. 15 Shop. Just look at all those driving belts and not a safety cover in sight!

The top foundry. Here there is a multitude of castings, weights, shovels, boxes and what is probably sand. No doubt this was a dirty place in which to work.

The paint shop displaying newly painted machines in pristine condition. This paint shop was used for engines and agricultural products, hence the number of Hornsby force feed machines awaiting despatch.

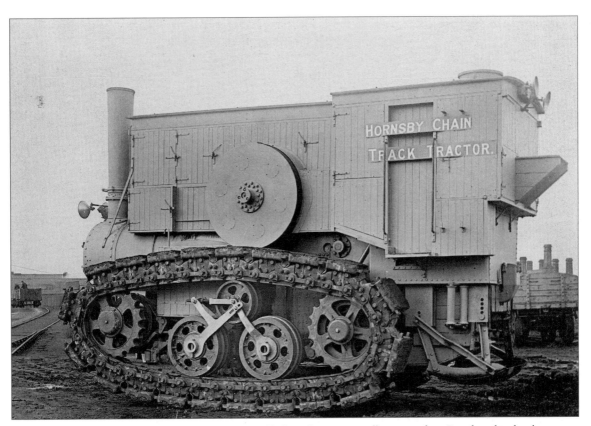

The Hornsby chain track tractor. The 'caterpillar' track was originally invented in Grantham but by the time it was really needed during the First World War the patent had been sold to a firm in the United States. This machine is steam driven and dates from about 1908. The boiler was made by William Foster & Co. of Lincoln.

The Power Lift tractor mower, *c.* 1936. This was designed by Mr A.E. Kitchen and patented by Ruston & Hornsby. Mr Kitchen later worked at R.H. Neal and then as works engineer at Coles Cranes. In this photograph, the driver is Mr Tommy Roberts.

An advertisement for the Grantham Boiler &
Crank Co., who were located in Dysart Road
between the two railway bridges. They were
established in 1885 and closed down in the mid-
1950s.

Another lost industry of Grantham is the Grantham
Steam Laundry along Belton Lane. It was opened in
September 1878 during Grantham's great
expansion years.

A steam traction engine rumbles by the top of Vine Street with no sign of smoke or smuts coming from the chimney. This photograph probably dates from the turn of this century.

Bjorlow (Great Britain) Ltd were situated alongside the Grantham–Nottingham canal and were involved with the preparation of leather. The site was previously occupied by Shaws' Tanneries Ltd, leather dressers.

The original Bjorlow factory in March 1974, which was then being used by Coles Cranes on Dysart Road. The building had previously been home to A.C. Potter & Co., but after they closed down in the 1930s, Messrs R.H. Neal, crane makers from Ealing, took over in 1937. They were later incorporated into Coles Cranes.

A detail of the brickwork along the wall facing Dysart Road. This photograph was taken in March 1974.

The rear of the main building clearly shows the name of the previous owner, Potter Pumps, Engineers, painted on the north-facing wall.

Neal's main assembly shop in 1962. Here numerous small cranes are under construction.

Neal's cranes in production in 1938. This is a Neal crane type F which had a 1 ton lifting capacity.

An aerial view of Neal's Dysart Road works in 1962. This photograph was taken some years before the great expansion that followed the takeover by Coles Cranes.

Shown here are the various cranes built by Neal's or Coles when Grantham had an important crane-building industry. The Neal's Hymax was a long-armed crane and 'run about'. This was used to reach into the awkward places that other cranes could not enter. Notice the bicycles ready for a quick getaway at 'home time'.

One of the many lorry-mounted cranes built by R.H. Neal and supplied to the Ministry of Defence. This model was photographed at the Dysart Road works. The chimneys of the houses on Greenhill Road are visible in the distance.

A very popular Coles crane during the 1970s; a Grantham-built rough terrain Husky 620. The Coles offices are visible in the background.

A Neal NS45 straight channel jib crane photographed in the early 1960s, handling scrap metal with an electromagnet at the Dysart Road works.

A restored Neal crane, type QM, at the main entrance to the works, on Dysart Road in the 1970s/80s. This crane was originally owned and worked by Aveling-Barford.

A nice shot of two of Grantham's products working together in the early 1960s, a Neal crane and an Aveling-Barford SF 3 cubic yard dumper.

A publicity photograph of a 15 ton Neal crane type NS 150 posed outside the Dysart Road works in the late 1950s.

Another popular Husky crane, the 150T, once again destined for the Ministry of Defence. The driver is Mr Stan Norman. The houses behind are in Greenhill Road off Barrowby Road.

The heaviest of the Aveling-Barford G series road rollers was the GD. It could weigh up to 16 tons, but rarely did, as its working weight was usually between 12 and 14 tons. Initially these rollers were fitted with an awning, but ETY 939, photographed outside the gatehouse at Denton in the early 1950s, was fitted with a very attractive and draught-proof cab.

The spacious and well-laid-out Aveling-Barford heavy machine shop at the Houghton Road factory. All the photographs of the Aveling-Barford workshops were taken during the early 1950s; certainly before 1952.

The roller erection shop. The rollers being built here are type GD, the heaviest of the superb G (for Grantham) series. This series was designed towards the end of the Second World War and the rollers were ready for the rebuilding of war-torn Britain and Europe.

A long line of motor graders under construction. They appear to be the original Aveling-Austin 99H.

An Aveling-Austin 99H motor grader on show at the Public Works and Municipal Exhibition in London, November 1950. This grader was built under licence from the Austin-Western Company of Aurora, Illinois.

The smallest of the G series, the type GA. It was used as a footpath roller or, when fitted with wider wheels, a sports-field roller.

Another of the new postwar designs was the Calfdozer, a miniature bulldozer. Several thousand were built. It worked in ships' holds, coal depots and building sites and was claimed to equal the output of ten men in back-filling trenches.

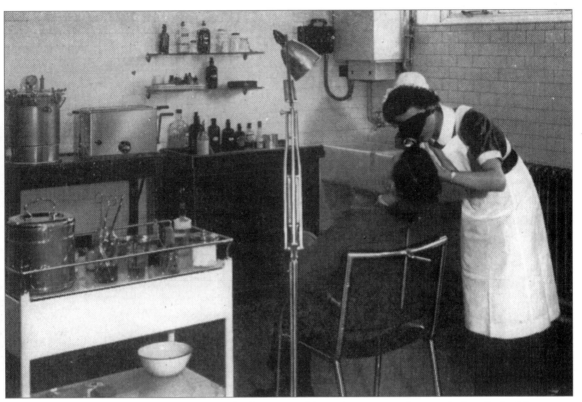

All good work places have their own medical centre, and Sister Stow was in charge at Aveling-Barford for many years.

A quiet and peaceful view, this time of Guildhall Street when Hiltons, the boot and shoe shop, was still there.

These buildings near the main railway bridge on Dysart Road are gone and almost forgotten especially now that an inner relief road is being constructed. The author recalls the Corporation street-cleaning carts being kept there and took the photograph in 1974.

The narrow medieval streets of Grantham cause daily headaches for drivers. This is what Elmer Street North and Swinegate looked like in more peaceful days. Notice that the stabling for the Angel & Royal Hotel is still standing and the sadly missed clock is visible.

The Queen Victoria Memorial Building in Castlegate. This building, which is still in existence, was originally built to house district nurses. This postcard was produced not long after the house was built in the Edwardian era.

Castlegate and the Beehive public house; surely a
scene from the 1930s. This was one of Grantham's
most unusual sights with its 'living sign' – a hive
full of bees. St Wulfram's church spire can clearly
be seen in the distance.

The postcard describes this scene as 'Grantham from Barrowby Road'. Actually all that can really be seen
is the railway embankment which carried the main line to the north and the branch line to Nottingham. It
still does so today.

This bridge on Dysart Road was for the first railway through Grantham in 1850 – the line to Nottingham. The bridge was demolished in September 1979. During the war, anti-blast walls were constructed on the footpath.

Another view of the same bridge, looking up Dysart Road towards Earlesfield.

North Parade in the early 1980s. This was the birthplace of Grantham's famous lady, Margaret Hilda Thatcher (née Roberts), who went on to develop a great career in politics.

A perfect shot of the famous corner shop.

Three cars moving, so it must be a busy place; it is even busier now. On the right is the famous corner shop belonging to Mr Alfred Roberts whilst the road ahead is the A52 main road to Nottingham. On the left now is Premier Court (also see p. 48), the name commemorating Mrs Thatcher and her premiership.

Beacon Lane leading up to Hall's Hill. Notice the postman with his bicycle. This picture is from a postcard mailed in Grantham on 24 March 1913.

Edward Street from a card posted in Grantham in May 1917. There is not a vehicle in sight, just children posing quite safely in the middle of the street for the photographer.

Grantham seen from about halfway down Gonerby Hill. Not much of Grantham is visible as only the streets with their Boer War names had been built in that area. Today, large numbers of houses are at present being built between Gonerby Road and Barrowby Road.

London Road looking south with the newly built Salvation Army Citadel on the right. The Citadel was opened in May 1896.

London Road looking south again, but this time nearer to the Wharf Road junction.

A tranquil scene showing London Road and looking towards St Peter's Hill. Again there is not a vehicle in sight in this Edwardian picture.

Tomlinson the hairdressers, or was it just a plain barber-shop in those days? Notice the two barber's poles; there are not many of these about now. This shop was in Vine Street and the building is still in use, but now as a Chinese take-away.

Looking south in Swinegate during 1906. Here it seems the photographer was the attraction.

What is most remarkable about this postcard is not the interesting scene of St Anne's Street and school area of Grantham but the message that is wishing the recipient a Merry Christmas for 1906. The card was posted in Grantham on Christmas Eve to an address in Cambridgeshire, and it was fully expected to arrive on Christmas Day.

This is a 'calling card' from Ellis Bros of 93 Westgate. It had been left at the home of Miss Burchnell of Skillington at 11 am on 8 August 1906 by Mr R. Bembridge, an Ellis Bros representative, who would call again the next day.

Heavily disguised and hiding behind the flat front are some very old houses in Wide Westgate. Also just in the picture is one of the town's well-remembered eating and meeting places, 'Phil's Grill', which was a very popular place years ago. It was owned by Phil Watkins who was a successful racing motor cyclist.

Narrow Westgate and the Blue Ram public house. This pub has now reverted to its original name of the King's Arms. It had that name in the eighteenth century, but became one of Grantham's 'Blue' pubs in the early 1800s. A quote from 'Our Old Nobility' throws some light on the reason for so many 'Blue' pubs. In 1802 Grantham had two Members of Parliament and was classed as a Pocket Borough, each MP being 'in the pocket' of one of the two nearby landed gentry. At the election that year the Manners family, wishing to show their power, had their public house names amended to Blue; hence the Green Man became Blue, the White Lion became Blue, and the King's Arms became the Blue Ram. Votes cost ten guineas each!

Narrow Westgate looking towards the market-place, *c.* 1913. Notice the definite curve of the street. Most people do not realize Westgate has such a bend in it but it is clearly shown here. The street probably follows the course of the nearby underground stream, the Mowbeck.

Westgate again but this time looking west from the market-place. This view is believed to date from the late 1930s.

The author has many childhood memories of this shop, as his father was manager here from 1928 until he retired owing to poor health in 1963. 'Easiephit' was the trade name of the Scottish firm Greenlees and Sons, and they opened this shop late in 1928 when Mr W.G. Knapp came from Leicester to become the first manager. This was a publicity photograph taken just after the new, larger lettering had been fitted. The photographer was *Boaz* of 17 Market Place.

The imposing houses in North Street. This is the little street between Watergate and North Parade. The motor-bike is parked at the entrance to James Street, another lost street.

Part of North Street from the other direction. It is thought that this photograph was taken in 1964.

North Street again. These buildings disappeared before Premier Court was built. Mr Cross was a shoe repairer who also sold second-hand books: a very useful shop for local historians who walk a lot.

The corner of Brownlow Street and Broad Street. All of this has disappeared and has been replaced by Premier Court, which is a very pleasant development for elderly people.

A lost street which has been swallowed up in the Isaac Newton shopping centre development and replaced by the car park. This was Rutland Street where most of the houses still had their shutters, even in 1974.

Barrowby Road looking towards the main line railway bridge. This is where the controversial inner relief road is being built and the first casualties were most of the trees. This is an early twentieth-century postcard scene.

This was the shop of White & Sentance, dealers in music, which has now gone and has been replaced by a large and ugly building. They sold wirelesses, records, pianos, organs, gramophones and needles and eventually television sets. This shop was on St Peter's Hill.

The Market Cross as it is not seen today. Standing alone in the middle of what is now a car park, it is majestic and imposing in its simplicity. The cross itself dates from *c.* 1280. The building behind is yet another 'Blue' pub, the Blue Lion, which was originally called the White Lion.

The Market Cross in all its medieval glory. Behind it is another of the lost 'Blue' pubs, the Blue Sheep. Notice the very narrow Conduit Lane between the pub and the Conduit. The building on the other side of the Blue Sheep is the old Butter Market, which was later used as a store room for the market stalls. It was built in 1872.

The market-place again but showing a different building, which was built in 1904 and dated to tell us so. This was therefore photographed between 1904 and 1910–11, as the Market Cross was restored to its rightful place in January 1911.

The market-place with its Aberdeen granite obelisk. It is difficult to date photographs like this precisely unless the photographer wished to assist future local historians by supplying a date. This scene can be dated to before 1904 and is possibly Edwardian.

This is one of the earliest photographs of the market-place and could date from the 1880s.

A much later photograph of the market-place. This was probably taken on a Saturday after the market, hence the rubbish.

High Street at a busy moment with two carts on the road. Actually, one is blurred so it must have been overtaking at speed! Fred Smith was mine host at the Horse and Jockey and although this pub seemed to be the wrong way round to the High Street as the entrance was down the passageway to the Horse and Jockey yard. However, this did not seem to discourage potential customers.

This imposing building housed the Grantham Co-operative Society. This was the main building and had numerous departments at street level with the offices and Committee room upstairs. The Co-op was established in Grantham in 1872 although the date stone states 1873. The building which was erected in 1884 has recently been renovated, and is now a large pub and restaurant named the 'Tollemache' – because of its proximity to the Tollemache statue on St Peter's Hill.

St Peter's Hill from the vantage point of the general post office roof with numerous vehicles and the spire of St Wulfram's Church visible. This is an early 1950s postcard.

This delightful view of St Peter's Hill was captured by Walter Lee probably just before the war started. The railings are there and there is even a tree almost outside the State cinema. All this is now gone.

A longer view of St Peter's Hill with the general post office on the left. This is not the present box-like building but one that was attractive to look at. It was probably not as efficient as today's, however. This is a 1960s photograph as the Post Office building seen here was replaced in 1969.

The Tollemache statue at the south end of St Peter's Hill, *c.* 1930. It was unveiled in March 1892.

Another view of Frederick Tollemache, who was MP for Grantham from 1826 to 1874. He died in 1888.

Two old and well-loved buildings. The Picture House, built during the First World War, was demolished in the 1960s. The Rainbow Café was another popular 'meeting and eating' establishment for many of Grantham's teenagers in the 1950s and 1960s.

The end of The Picture House from a photograph probably taken in May 1961. As can be seen, the site of The Picture House is now only an empty space between two other buildings.

All has changed and even the State cinema is now the Granada. The Picture House is still an empty space.

High Street during the First World War. The message on the postcard mailed in April 1915 by a soldier at Belton Camp was that Grantham was 'a decent town' and that 'he had a fairly good billet in George Street 1½ miles from the range'.

The Granada with the Guildhall Tavern next door. One of Grantham's photographers is remembered here as the shop and studio of John Mackay are next to the cinema. Walter Lee has also had a business in that shop. The Granada screened its last film in April 1972.

This is High Street looking north with Harrisons, the printers and stationers, clearly visible. These long-lost buildings are much more attractive compared with what we have now.

Remember Mr Wallace the dentist next door to Bradley's Almshouses? These were built in 1875 at a cost of £1,300. Southwards was Spouge, the sweet and ice-cream shop, followed by Cresswell the butcher. Here there was even a policeman on the beat. This photograph was taken in around 1961.

Going north and next door to the Almshouses was J. Porter & Son, a long-established boot and shoe shop and repairer. The business was founded in 1829. Again, this photograph dates from around 1961.

Another late lamented building, whose loss is even greater if one looks at what has replaced this late Georgian façade. The Red Lion Hotel was a very useful medium-sized town centre hotel. It also had a very popular bar.

The High Street entrance to the Red Lion Hotel. The Hotel closed in 1961.

A night-time view of the floodlit front of the Red Lion, presumably a 1950s publicity photograph. This is from a hotel postcard giving the address and two telephone numbers, Grantham 170 and 1236.

The Horse and Jockey and the Georgian buildings next door. The beautiful doorway is still there. The chemist was Calvert's. As the Horse and Jockey pub closed in May 1958 this photograph, probably taken by Walter Lee, must date from the early 1950s.

High Street looking south from outside the George Hotel, *c.* 1920. Notice that the pathway outside the hotel is kerbed to allow the horse-drawn vehicles to enter into the courtyard.

High Street but this time looking north. Notice the iron railings outside the buildings on the right. On the left is Waterloo House in all its glory; this was when Grantham possessed a department store of its own. As the iron railings are still standing, this scene must date from before 1939.

An earlier postcard of High Street again showing Waterloo House, probably in the 1900s. The boys are wearing their knickerbocker trousers which gives an indication of the date.

This is included to recall another of Grantham's local businesses, G.W. Green and Son who were at 49–51 High Street. The firm was established in 1911 and were 'General Drapers' and children's outfitters; the type of shop we apparently lack today.

A fine view of the George Hotel and High Street with traffic. The pavement is now complete and the entrance to the courtyard has been blocked off. The well-remembered revolving doors had now been fitted.

The other hotel. This was the Angel & Royal Hotel on the other side of High Street but not quite opposite the George. This is one of the oldest inns in England and has seen many important people and historical events. Boot's the chemists were next door.

Watergate looking north on a card posted in Grantham in May 1917. The writer of the message stated '2,000 men on Church Parade with a splendid band'. Just notice how narrow the top of Watergate really was. It looks narrow even when only one boy is standing in it, which makes it hard to realize that this was the Great North Road.

This is the top of the much widened Watergate, with the gentlemens outfitters 'Weaver to Wearer' prominent at the top of the street.

Watergate still looking north but now further down the street. This area used to be one of Grantham's busiest shopping streets, and while some shops remain, the largest area is now a plain but useful car park.

The widening process continued and the top of Watergate and part of Vine Street are now gone. Later an attractive garden was established in this area before the present unattractive shops were built. The whole process started in 1948.

Still Watergate, and at this time in the 1950s full of useful shops, often in Georgian or pre-Georgian buildings.

W.B. Harrison and Sons, manufacturers of Art Wicker and Cane Furniture occupied the tallest building shown here. Next door were the offices of the West Kesteven Rural District Council and the Registry Office. All of this is now only a memory and was opposite what is now the large Watergate car park.

Further down Wharf Road and a boarded-up Fred Bates shop, *c.* 1977. Many Grantham men will recall with great pleasure all the fishing tackle that could be obtained from the Bates shop. Originally the building had been the Temperance Hall and was built in 1874.

W.F. Swallow & Son's Spitalgate Watermill at the south end of town on the River Witham. The building is still there but it is no longer a watermill. It was a night-club for some time.

About 2 miles out of Grantham on the A52 going towards Boston is this stone building. At the time of the photograph it was the Blue Harbour pub but was previously known as Cold Harbour, probably denoting previous Roman occupation on the site. The term 'Cold Harbour' regularly appears on Roman roads, and was probably an overnight camping site along one of their long, straight routes. The information with the card suggests it was 'Dick Turpin's House of Call'. What can be said with more certainty is that it stands at the meeting point of the Roman Ermine Street and the pre-Roman trackway known as the Saltway. Salterfords Road in Grantham is part of that same ancient salt route.

Impressive houses on Dudley Road. They were at one time the YHA hostel in Grantham but they are now combined into the Birchwood Retirement Home.

Turnor Crescent. This housing scheme was the brain child of Mr Christopher Hatton Turnor JP who was Mayor of Grantham, 1928–1930. It comprised sixty-four houses at a rent of 4s per week with four new roads, one appropriately named Turnor Crescent. At the time of the scheme in 1930, Councillor Harry Beeden was Chairman of the Housing Committee. He was later to have Beeden Park, at the top of Dysart Road, named after him.

Branch No. 8 of the Grantham Co-operative Society. This branch was on Dysart Road and was the Earlesfield shop. It was officially opened in August 1926 and closed down in November 1994. The Grantham Co-op had numerous shops in and around the town and in nearby local villages. One can always remember one's Co-op check number. My mother's was 1371 and ours 5101. Do you remember yours?

Grantham Carriage Works on St Peter's Hill. Not many people, as they walk down the passageway of the Isaac Newton Centre, will realize they are in fact going down to the site of the Grantham Carriage Works, unless they notice the initials carved in stone that have been incorporated into the brickwork.

George Street and the Empire Theatre just after it had been closed down in 1962. The theatre was built in 1875 but was destroyed by fire in 1888. It was rebuilt in 1890.

The former *Grantham Journal* offices. Originally the building was the Mail Hotel and was one of the stopping places for the Mail or Stage coaches (hence the name) as they came along the Great North Road in Georgian and early Victorian times. These buildings are again just a memory.

Part of the bus station, but more importantly the Grantham Borough Police Station. This was in use from 1929 to 1959.

The replacement for the old police station was 'Stonebridge', a mid-Victorian house situated on the east side of the River Witham. This was opened for the Lincolnshire police force on Monday 25 May 1959 just over 100 years after 'Stonebridge' was built in 1858.

The George Shopping Centre development, as seen from Westgate in 1991.

The scaffolding in Guildhall Street during the construction of the George Shopping Centre.

During the war it was decided that Grantham needed a bypass. There were rumblings that trade might be lost because of this, but eventually it became clear to everyone that one was needed. Now we need another! This view is of the Grantham bypass under construction and photographed from the Stroxton (pronounced Strawson) Road bridge in 1960.

The same road but photographed from the Little Ponton bridge.

The Conduit Intake House. This was in a field between Dysart Road and Barrowby Road but has now been totally destroyed by vandals. It was built over the spring that provided the fresh water for the Conduit in the market-place from 1314 onwards. This photograph was taken just after its restoration in 1930–1. It is not entirely clear whether the Intake house was a fourteenth- or a sixteenth-century building.

The Blue Cow, yet another of the 'Blue' pubs that are now no more. This pub was one of many in Castlegate and was demolished when Fine Fare built their supermarket in 1972. It actually closed as a pub in 1959.

The Borough of Grantham celebrated its Civic Centenary in 1935 with a big parade and shop window displays. Here, apparently leading the parade, is the Grantham Town Band followed by the Borough Fire Engine. The weather looks fair and there is a large crowd lining the route.

The same parade but a little later and showing more fire-fighting equipment.

Here comes the equipment made by the local firms. The tractor is towing some agricultural machinery, probably made by Ruston & Hornsby.

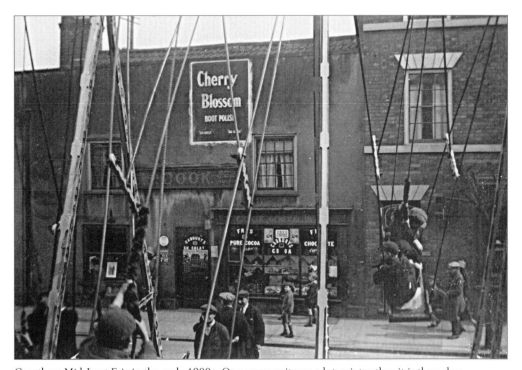

Grantham Mid-Lent Fair in the early 1900s. One assumes it was a lot quieter than it is these days.

An Armistice Day Parade formed outside the Guildhall on St Peter's Hill. This was when the Armistice Day ceremony was held on 11 November no matter what day of the week it fell on. Notice the dress of the Royal Air Force contingent, no doubt from RAF Spitalgate. The policeman is PC Bramhall who later became a detective in the Grantham Borough Police Force.

Armistice Sunday, 1954. The Colour Party are marching smartly towards the saluting base at the Guildhall. Those visible include Sgts. McWilliams and Streather and Cpl. Knapp, all of the 4th/6th Battalion Royal Lincolnshire Regiment (TA).

Grantham was blessed with two high-quality seed shops, but sadly both have closed. One was Chas. Sharpe & Co. Ltd, and the other was Ogdens. Sharpe's, who closed in 1986, were in business in Grantham for over 100 years. Both shops were in the market place and only about 30 yards apart. This is Ogdens, who were next door to the Conduit. Mr C.S. Cupit was the well-remembered and popular owner.

Some of the ladies of the Grantham & District Licensing Trade at their evening dinner at the George Hotel, *c.* 1950. Among the ladies are Mrs Murr of the Earlesfield Hotel, Mrs Palethorpe of the Horse & Jockey, Mrs Widdowson of the Blue Horse at Great Ponton, Mrs Lappage, Mrs Scott, Mrs Cadwallader, Mrs Philpotts and Mrs Burch.

Theo Rowle & Co. of 1 Vine Street. Mr Rowle and his assistant are posing in the shop doorway. This shop and business disappeared when Watergate was widened and that part of Vine Street was demolished.

The opening of the Princess Drive branch of the Grantham Co-operative Society. This event took place on the last Saturday in November 1956. It is now the only Co-op in Grantham and is part of the Greater Nottingham Co-operative Society.

The central grocery store of the Grantham Co-op. This was a publicity photograph taken just after the conversion to self service. It was the first self-service store in the town.

The popular tobacconist Gordon Foster, shown here, must have bought himself a nice new van in the summer of 1922 and had a publicity photograph taken to celebrate the event.

The name of Cant was well known in Grantham as a hairdresser from the 1850s and it was a business that passed down from father to son. This is Mr Stephen Cant outside his shop at 60 Westgate, probably during the First World War. It is now a Chinese restaurant.

High-Class MEAT AT Popular Prices !

Prime Chilled Beef, from
$3\frac{1}{2}$d. to $6\frac{1}{2}$d.

Selected Wether Mutton, from
$3\frac{1}{2}$d. to 6d.

Canterbury Lamb, from
$7\frac{1}{2}$d. to $8\frac{1}{2}$d.

PLEASE NOTE THE ADDRESS :

The River Plate Fresh Meat Co.
Ltd.,
26 MARKET PLACE, GRANTHAM.

An advertising card for The River Plate Fresh Meat Co. Unfortunately it is not dated.

BRITISH STOCK THE STANDARD QUALITY ! ! !

The reverse of the same card. This company obviously had connections with the beef trade in South America, but how fresh it was after travelling from there is questionable.

They were even digging up the roads in the early 1900s, so nothing has changed. This is just outside the Angel & Royal Hotel, at the top of Vine Street. Messrs Callender & Co. were the contractors, so they may have been laying cables but it looks more like water pipes.

A very early view of engines at Grantham Station from a painting that was later produced as a postcard. These are three different types designed by the Great Northern Railway designer Mr Patrick Stirling. Stirling Court in Grantham is named after him. This is probably an artist's view from around 1900.

A delightfully atmospheric photograph, taken by Terry Shelbourne, of the Goods yard at Grantham railway station. The train pictured here was called 'Enterprise' and was a class A3 (4–6–2), number 60111. It looks as though it needed a good clean.

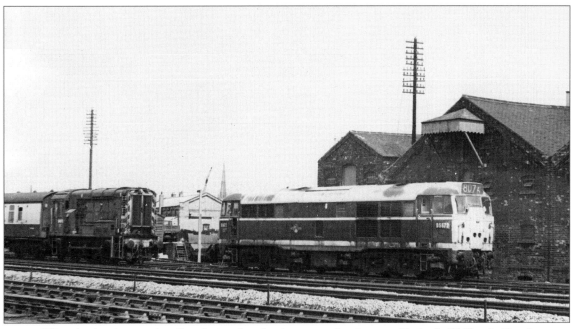

When the diesels arrived at Grantham, a lot of train spotters lost interest. Notice St Wulfram's Church spire peeping over the rear of diesel D5872.

A much loved Grantham doctor for many years was Dr Charles Frier. His surgery was in Spitalgate House on London Road, and he was the founder of the charity that started in the 1920s which sent children from poor Grantham families on a holiday to the seaside at Skegness.

Dr Charles Haldane Denny Robbs, another of Grantham's well-remembered doctors, had his home and surgery in 5 Vine Street. After all these years it is once again a doctor's surgery.

Miss H. Gladys Williams was the headmistress of the Kesteven & Grantham Girls School (KGGS) when it opened in 1910. She remained in charge there until 1939 when Miss Dorothy J.C. Gillies took over. Miss Williams died in 1968. The school opened in September 1910 with 102 pupils, this number growing over the years, and has had many very successful students, including one who became our Prime Minister.

Mr William Joseph Huggins, the no-nonsense headmaster of the King's School from 1939 to 1958. A plaque to his memory was unveiled in the Old School in 1991 which bears his maxim, 'work hard and play hard'. The author has no unpleasant memories of the 'Old Man', as one quickly learned to keep out of his way.

A First World War wedding which took place in August 1915 at St John's Church. This shows the reception in Inner Street and the happy couple who were Mr and Mrs Palethorpe. Later they were greatly involved with the Grantham Licensing Trade.

A very smart turn-out of the Richard Hornsby Fire Brigade. This photograph is not dated. 'The Firm' had its own fire brigade which was totally separate from that of the Borough.

The Grantham Town football team during their very successful season of 1937–8. Harry Pringle was the trainer. He later worked with the author at Aveling-Barford. Arthur Jepson was the goalkeeper and eventually played in the Football League. He was also a fast bowler for Nottinghamshire. The team were runners-up to Shrewsbury Town in the Midland League at the end of this exciting season.

Remembering Mr Huggins and his 'work hard and play hard' motto, this is the King's School First Cricket XI in 1946. There were some quite good performers in the team, including Jeff Carpenter and captain Keith Castings who tragically died at a very early age. P.G.E. (Peggy) Griffin was a good trier and was the author's House Captain.

Grantham Borough officials all looking very smart in uniform. The Town's maces are being carried by members of the Grantham Borough Police. The maces are at present being repaired and re-gilded at a cost of £4,000. Mr Tryner Lynn was Mayor of Grantham in the Mayoral year 1900–1 so this august and sombre looking gathering is probably announcing that Queen Victoria is dead, and proclaiming 'Long Live King Edward VII'. Other notables in the picture include Chief Constable John R. Casburn, Mr Handley-Parker, Canon Glaister and Mr Gamble.

The Salvation Army always had a high presence in the town, especially after the imposing Citadel was built. This photograph shows Mr and Mrs Sims in uniform with their family in 1931.

The Mayor and Corporation of the Borough of Grantham in 1935 when Lord Brownlow was the Mayor. As usual these official photographs were taken in front of the Guildhall.

A similar photograph taken two years later in 1937. In this Coronation year, Alderman Arthur Eatch was Mayor.

Lord Baden-Powell came to the Lincolnshire Scouts Rally in August 1925. Here he is shown addressing the large assembly gathered to greet him.

This time Lord Baden-Powell is on 'walkabout' among the scouts and is accompanied by the host Lord Brownlow, as the rally was in Belton Park, and Captain Reeve.

Councillor Alfred Roberts photographed when chairman of the 1937 Coronation Celebration Finance Sub-Committee. Later, during the war, he held other positions; he became an Alderman and was also Mayor of Grantham. He balanced this career with having a thriving corner shop and being the father of Margaret very successfully.

William Bradshaw JP in 1921. Mr Bradshaw, born in 1876, was brought into the Grantham Co-op in 1903 to sort out its affairs and put it on a successful footing. The Society had encountered a lot of opposition from local traders and was struggling to survive. He succeeded in this venture and was later knighted for his work in the Co-operative movement. For many years he lived at 79 Harrowby Road.

This is the earliest photograph to be found before the closure of the Co-op buildings on St Catherine's Road as apparently most of the others were lost. This is an important picture of the Management Committee during the Society's Jubilee Anniversary in 1922. William Bradshaw is in the centre of the front row. On the back row are Messrs Robinson, King, Henderson, Parker, Leadbeter and Barnes, and on the front row are Messrs Woodruff, Coldron, Sutton and Needham.

All Committees like to have their photograph taken for posterity and the Management Committee of the Grantham Co-operative Society in 1950 was no exception. This shows Alderman Walter H. Dale JP as their President; he was also the Mayor of Grantham. Councillor Leonard Audus was Secretary and General Manager.

The year is 1955–6 and now Alderman Leonard Audus JP is Mayor as well as the Secretary and General Manager. It was he who was responsible for the introduction of the self-service system into the supermarket that was mentioned earlier.

The date of this committee is 1966–7 and shows a few different faces and yet another Co-op member as Mayor of Grantham. Montague 'Monty' Ogden now holds this office.

All large organizations that have numerous vehicle drivers like to encourage good driving. This includes such organizations as the Post Office (now the Royal Mail), the Railway Company (before nationalization in Grantham it was the LNER) and the Co-op. Here are the winners of the Grantham Co-op 'Safe Driving Awards' after the presentation by another Mayor of Grantham, Councillor J.R. 'Bob' Cook. He was Mayor in 1967–8.

It is prize night for the Angling Section of R.H. Neal, the crane makers, with one of the Neal brothers sitting behind the prizes. Also in the group is Mr Ward, the Works Manager, and Mr H.S. 'Cub' Kemp. He was nicknamed 'Cub' because of his many years in the Scout movement from a very early age.

The 'Loyal Hutchinson Female Lodge of the Manchester Unity of Odd Fellows'. This is a members' party held in about 1933 at Stonebridge which was then the home of Mrs Schwind, née Miss Hutchinson, and her husband. It is now the police station.

A class of angelic little girls all (well, nearly all) dressed up in their spotlessly clean aprons at the Inner Street Mission Room School, c. 1905.

The General Knowledge team representing Grantham in 1966 in the Anglia TV Quiz named 'Contest' which took place at Norwich. Grantham won the first round when Spalding were beaten in a frantic finish, but that was their only moment of glory. The second round was lost. The team was Geoff Winter, Malcolm Knapp, David Butler and George Mitcham.

Form IV of the Girls Secondary Modern School, *c.* 1948–9. This was more usually known in town as the Grantham Girls' Central School of Castlegate. Mrs Joyce Dickin, in the white overall, was the cookery teacher and Mrs Eileen Smith was in charge of needlework. Names of some of the girls include Pat Turner, Janet Smith, Janet Green, June Toulson, Dorothy Woolley, June Marriott, Doreen Haddock, Beatrice Crowe and Gillian Knapp.

'The Intrepids' in the late 1960s. The group included Colin Haddock, John Smith, Keith Maxon, Bob Leeson and Gerald Saddington who was the vocalist. The inclusion of this group is made so that all the other Grantham groups including The Vagabonds, The Pontiacs, The Kobolts, and The Delcounts can be recalled with pleasure. Let us not forget that one young man from Grantham, Brian Locking, joined The Shadows.

The 'Pete Smith Sound', *c.* 1973. This is at a Christmas Dinner Dance at the George Hotel. Ron Haddock is the trumpeter, John Hedworth played guitar and Pete Smith is the leader and keyboard player. Despite repeated enquiries, the name of the drummer is unknown.

The favourite backcloth of the Guildhall once more but this time it is the B. Marco Band, with Conductor/Band Master Harry Sale and Drum Major Tom Adams, that is the subject of the photographer. The Band has had many names during its lifetime and was called the B. Marco Band because that was where it could practise. It is now known as the Grantham Concert Band.

The Grantham Wesleyan School in 1927. This school was in Wharf Road and the building has recently been demolished to make way for some flats. Also on this site was the Chapel with a burial ground, the first burial having been in 1835. Some of the Chapel plaques are being relocated to the Methodist Church in Finkin Street.

'Export or else'. Something like this was the 'in' phrase in the 1950s and here is a 'trainful' of Hotpoint Washing Machines off to Australia. They were specially packed for their long journey by Barrett Packaging Ltd, of Grantham, who are no longer in business.

Heading south to King's Cross. This is class V2 60800 'Green Arrow' steaming under the South Parade bridge with an 'Up' Express. This was during the halcyon days of steam when Grantham was a very important steam engine depot.

Many residents of Grantham have no idea that there is a burial ground on Manthorpe Road. It used to be visible from the top of double-decker buses, but the trees and bushes planted by Mr Jauch have now grown up and hidden it. It was an 'overspill' cemetery used after the burial ground around St Wulfram's Church was filled up. It is opposite the Waggon & Horses public house.

A wartime photograph of the wreath laying ceremony at the monument to Sir Isaac Newton, a King's School old boy, in December 1942. This particular event celebrated Sir Isaac's 300th birthday. Notice the defences in front of the Guildhall and that all the cast-iron railings have gone for scrap.

Not a particularly clear photograph but it does illustrate some of the traffic problems that occurred after our American allies arrived and found they had to drive on the other side of the road! This does not look like a serious accident but no doubt the car driver was a bit surprised. Probably the American GI was equally shocked when the car suddenly appeared on his 'wrong side'.

A closer view of the 'shunt' which happened at the junction of Westgate, Wharf Road, and Station Road. With all those roads coming together it did help to have several pairs of eyes. Notice the railway carriage on the Station Road embankment.

Grantham Market on a Saturday in 1944. In its original form this photograph is in colour and is a 35mm slide taken by an American Army Air Force Officer. He was stationed in Grantham and, in fact, lived at the George Hotel. An American Jeep is parked among the market stalls.

The Blue Pig and Swinegate, *c.* 1944. Notice the two air raid shelters further down the street. This is also a 35mm colour slide and was taken by Major (later Lt. Col.) James Mandigo of the USAAF.

During the invasion scare of 1940 and later in 1941, many men volunteered to join the Home Guard. This photograph, taken by Walter Lee in 1941, is of No. 1 Platoon of the 3rd Kesteven Battalion Home Guard. Lt. Jack Broadbent was in command with 2nd Lt. C. Statham MC as his second-in-command. The platoon sergeant was Sgt. M. Jackson.

This photograph of the Special Constabulary was taken by Walter Lee in 1943. This was the Borough of Grantham contingent. Mr W. Weatherhogg was the Chief Constable, Mr H.S. Appleby was the Commandant, who was assisted by Inspector G.W.C. Curry of the Grantham Borough Police.

This happy group was on a visit to the Guinness Brewery, Park Royal, London. It was an outing in August 1967 by the Grantham and District Ladies Licensed Trade Auxiliary. Among those smiling faces are Jack and Lil Smith, Ivy Geddes, Trixie Bunting, Marion Widdowson, Katie Palethorpe, Rex Pulfrey, 'Bubby' Haines, Phoebe Cadwallader, Sam and Eileen Hardy. They all appear to have had a very good time.

The busy Grantham bus station. This has now gone as the Council Offices of South Kesteven District Council have taken up the space, and the new bus station is on Wharf Road. The first platform next to the kiosk was for Lincolnshire Road Car or Trent buses going to Nottingham. To be precise it was signposted as the Omnibus Station but no one ever called it that.

The Carrier Assembly Shop. During the Second World War the factories of Grantham went over to making all types of armaments for the war effort. Aveling-Barford produced Bren gun carriers and eventually production reached a peak of sixty per week. The first vehicle underwent its tests in May 1939 about four months before the war started.

Cribbage was a very popular game played in pubs. Leagues were organized and trophies fiercely contested. In 1947–8 the Earlesfield Hotel team were the League winners. Mr Frank 'Sid' Smith was the captain and George Murr was the landlord host at the pub which is now named The Priory. Others in the winning team include Gordon Drake, W.O. Hodgkins RAF and Messrs Dexter and Shutt.

Some of Grantham's beautiful young ladies in 1953. This was the year of the Queen's Coronation and when Grantham had its Coronation Queen contest. Several of these pretty ladies still live in or around the town. Their names are Mrs Wilde and Misses Mumby, Osbourne, Rogers, Bowley and Geddes.

A Richard Hornsby & Son boundary stone. This was spotted by Don Brandom near the South Parade railway bridge. Hornsby's must have erected these boundary stones around their property in 1902, and this one is still *in situ*. The question is, are there any more still in existence?

Jollifications or celebrations outside the Wheatsheaf pub in Inner Street, 1935. This pub closed in 1938. There is a conflict of opinions as to what they were all celebrating but it was either that Inner Street had won the decorated street competition for the Civic Celebrations hands down or they were all celebrating King George V's Silver Jubilee.

The Blue Pig on the corner of Vine Street and Swinegate. Not much has changed since this photograph, but what is unusual is that the photographer was the State cinema organist and wartime reserve police constable, Lewis Gerrard. His real name was Gerrard Lewis.

Grantham Market Place in 1805. Whether this a true painting of the market place or whether there has been some artistic licence exercised here is not clear. Certainly the width of the street opening showing the Angel Inn, its name in 1805, appears too great. Nevertheless it is an interesting painting with plenty going on.

The window display in the shop of Stephen Cant, the hairdresser, at 60 Westgate. This is a publicity postcard from the 1930s.

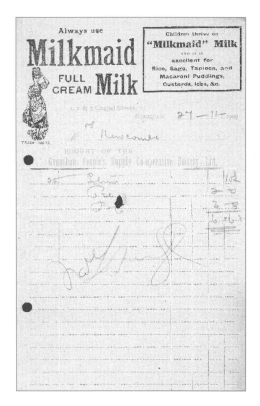

A 1909 receipt from the Grantham People's Supply Co-operative Society of 1, 2 and 3 Chapel Street. Even Chapel Street has gone now!

All the names have changed in this part of Grantham, seen *c*. 1970. Along this section of St Peter's Hill was the Granada cinema and the shops of John Mackay, White & Sentance and the old building used by the Westminster Bank. All have now gone including the Zebra crossing.

High Street, and showing what was later to be known as Lloyds Bank corner. This is before their new bank was built and the bunting is to celebrate the Coronation of Edward VII.

Advertisements, especially those with prices on, are always worth looking at. This has no prices but nevertheless is still of interest as it shows how the Roberts Store took up Nos 1 to 3 in the North Parade. Business must have been good to pay for that kind of expansion.

The Grantham FC team were Midland League Champions in 1970–1. Terry Bly was the successful Manager and 'Pim' Taylor was the trainer after a long career as the 'Town's' centre-half. They are standing on the London Road ground which has now been replaced by another supermarket. Susan Izdebski is the Gala Queen.

February 1945 and the war will soon be over. Here are girls, plus the male charge-hand, from one of the factory bays at B. Marco, photographed by Walter Lee.

Newcome the pharmacist on High Street, was also the supplier of such things as paints, varnishes and paint brushes, plus horse and cattle medicines.

The market place with a nice collection of 1930s vehicles. Notice that F.W. Woolworth has arrived. The 'nothing over 3*d* & 6*d*' store came to Grantham in 1924.

These stone and brick houses in Old Wharf Road where photographed during the summer of 1971 just before they were demolished. They were presumably workers' cottages built after the Grantham–Nottingham Canal was opened in the 1790s or before Grantham's first railway was opened in 1850. The canal basin and the first railway station were both up Old Wharf Road.

Brownlow Street. The whole of this area was cleared when Vere Street and James Street were demolished as part of the slum clearing process. It was eventually replaced by Premier Court.

Dudley Road in the early 1900s.

The Waggon and Horses on Manthorpe
Road before the pub front was altered.

The Bee-Hive pub in Castlegate is happily still
there and supplying beer. This is a 1920s
photograph and shows the actual bee hive. No
doubt the supply of beer in the wooden barrels is
from Grantham's own brewers – Messrs
Mowbray & Co. Ltd.

A gathering on the Guildhall steps on VE Day to celebrate the end of the war in Europe with a short service. Mr Sims, of the Salvation Army, is here in uniform with his musical instrument. Councillor R.R. Dale is the Mayor.

A very early photograph of the Earlesfield County Primary School. The school opened just before the war and took children from the expanding Earlesfield district of Grantham. Miss N.F. Cant was the headmistress. She would be surprised to be told that the school had recently changed its name to the Earl of Dysart C.P. School.

Probably the first photograph taken in 1938 of the staff for the new school in Earlesfield. Miss Cant was assisted by her long time friend Mrs Eleanor Bates and Miss Nellie Tuxford. The name of the other lady teacher is not known. They are seated on the lawn by the veranda which was in front of the three classrooms.

These are the dinner ladies at Earlesfield School with the headmistress, now known as Mrs N.F. Goldner. Included in the group is a former Mayoress of Grantham, Mrs Ogden, the wife of Monty Ogden who is mentioned previously. This photograph was probably taken in the late 1960s or early 1970s.

Mrs Goldner is in the middle of the front row wearing her 'I'm in charge' look. And she certainly was. This is another photograph dating from the late 1960s.

This is another of the early photographs taken just after the school was opened. The veranda is alongside the large cloakroom and led to Miss Cant's office. Later, during the war, it led to the air raid shelters!

A dinner-time scene with the children 'helping' the dinner ladies. The photograph was taken in the early 1970s.

BRITAIN IN OLD PHOTOGRAPHS

To order any of these titles please telephone our distributor, Littlehampton Book Services on 01903 721596
For a catalogue of these and our other titles please ring Regina Schinner on 01453 731114